1994

To Gerry love
...

THE IRISH CARD

BRENDAN CLEARY

♣

THE
Irish
Card

BLOODAXE BOOKS

ISBN: 1 85224 258 2

First published 1993 by
Bloodaxe Books Ltd,
P.O. Box 1SN,
Newcastle upon Tyne NE99 1SN.

Bloodaxe Books Ltd acknowledges
the financial assistance of Northern Arts.

Cover printing by J. Thomson Colour Printers Ltd, Glasgow.

Printed in Great Britain by
Bell & Bain Limited, Glasgow, Scotland.

For Margaret O'Brien

Acknowledgements

Some of these poems were published in Brendan Cleary's pamphlets *The Party's Upstairs* (Smith/Doorstop, 1987), *Memos to Sensitive Eddie* (Wide Skirt Press, 1987), *Late Night Bouts* (Bad Seed Press, 1987), *Newcastle Is Benidorm* (Echo Room Press, 1988), *Crack* (Echo Room Press, 1990) and *Transylvania* (Echo Room Press, 1992), and in his collection *White Bread & ITV* (Wide Skirt Press, 1990).

Acknowledgements are also due to the editors of the following publications in which some of these poems first appeared: *Apples & Snakes: The Popular Front of Contemporary Poetry* (Apples & Snakes, 1992), *Bad Seed Review, The Echo Room, Foolscap, Gown Literary Supplement, Harry's Hand, High on the Walls: A Morden Tower Anthology* (Morden Tower/Bloodaxe Books, 1990), *Hybrid, Iron, Map Makers Colours: New Poets from Northern Ireland* (Nu-Age Editions, Montreal, 1988), *Melville's Dark Anus* (USA), *Newcastle Evening Chronicle, New England Review* (USA), *New Statesman, New Writing in the West* (Connacht Tribune), *The New Younger Irish Poets* (Blackstaff Press, 1991), *The North, Out From Beneath the Boot: An Anthology of Radical Poetry* (Neruda, Glasgow, 1992), *Poésie Europe* (Germany), *The Rialto, The Salmon, Scotia Bar Anthology* (Taranis Books, Glasgow, 1992), *Scratch, Small Times* (Australia), *Smith's Knoll, Smoke, Stand, The Steeple, Sunk Island Review, 12 Bar Blues: Raven Introduction 6* (Raven Arts, Dublin, 1990), *The Wide Skirt*, and *Wordworks* (Bloodaxe Books/Tyne Tees Television, 1992).

The author wishes to thank Bernard and Mary Loughlin at the Tyrone Guthrie Centre, Annaghmakerigg, Co. Monaghan, Ireland, where many of these poems were written, and Northern Arts for writers' bursaries awarded in 1988 and 1992.

Contents

THE IRISH CARD

MEMOS TO SENSITIVE EDDIE

Come off it

Eddie, Eddie, Eddie
when will you catch a grip?
You've lent yourself out
to some pretty dubious agencies
so what do you expect?
Only junk mail loves you now
piled up like spaghetti.

There are so many fruity invitations
if you match the lucky numbers, Eddie.
Meet the crew of Concorde
hang out with the Hairspray Brigade,
models in their clinging boob-tubes.
Go on, get trigger happy
with the mind expanding zoom lens
in the quaint back passages
in the cathedrals & plazas
of leaf-strewn European capitals.
It's all yours, Eddie, yours.
Try a taste of feeling fine
in some spineless kitchenette.
Saucepans, Eddie, with matching lids!

Go on, get yourself down
to the patio restaurant, Eddie
over expensive melon or prawn dips
become slick, irresistible to girls...

Eddie's Enigma

When barstools never stop enticing
forget the ambiguity of her smile.
You'll be poking up daisies in no time, Ed
if you let it all get you down.

Forget what she symbolises,
her promise of some endless globetrot,
the flavour of her kisses
on the windswept decks
of distant steamers.
It's all just fantasy, Ed
get that straight.
This isn't a Martini advert
so come on, come out of the ether.
Here's ink! Here's an application form!
SELL CAMERAS, SELL JUNK FOOD,
SELL VACUUM CLEANERS,
sell what you need to
but wise up & straighten out.
There's got to be a better world
than this soft-focus blur,
than harking after impossible definitions.
Her waist when she picks up underwear
in the first thud of sunlight,
her riot of brown hair...

Repeats

Still in love with Diana Rigg
in 1966 after all this time...
wise your scones, Eddie
she never dresses in leather
except for repeats
her karate chop is obsolete
and it's no good driftin & droolin
for christ's sake go out
find yourself a wife!

Look! if she did smile at you
in the Vegetarian Takeaway
if it was her, & I doubt it
forget it ever happened, Eddie
you & Diana Rigg, Eddie

I mean, Diana Rigg!
you & Diana Rigg in the barleyfields
in her luxurious bath
while Steed was in Morocco
aye, Eddie, sure thing
then you woke up
& had your Special K...

The sermon

Talk about substance destroyed
by riotous behaviour, Eddie
you're a walking chemical plant

You weighed in last night
guttered, out of your tree
wantin to know if I thought
you looked a bit like Adam Ant
more like Bugs Bunny, Eddie...

Your untrammelled rambling
drives me haywire, Eddie
how many checkout girls
want your autograph this month?

Look at the state of your eyes, Eddie
zippy pinheads!
do you have a heart
or only a hard-on?
why's it always the same sob story
about giros lost or overdue...

Number 27 in the book

So you wanted an angel
to show you youth, Eddie
a girl to blether on
about French painters
or Baudelaire to in the bath.
So you wanted a princess
to kick her high heels off
in a whim, run through the dew
of the glistening parkside.
So what, Eddie?
So what if she wanted a child
to name after a riotous summer
& you wanted daydreams
of daytrips forever?
So what.
What do you expect now
you're back off cloud 9, Eddie
a Blue Peter badge
a Crackerjack pencil...

'Cheap little floosies'

POWER
is that what it's all about, Eddie?
discuss...
power to pull the 'chicks'
the girls you've convinced yourself
dress for your advantage only
power to pull the 'dynamite blondes'
the 'big, brassy brunettes'
who, needless to say,
come 'lookin for it'.
I mean, if they don't want to wake up
next to your hangover,

your stinking feet & genitals
or even in the remote chance they do
you can always call them 'hussies'
after umpteen pints & ginflips
with those poisonous wee glipes
you call your best mates.
Down in the Glamour Trap
I've seen the lot of you
droolin about suspenders
all the frilly accessories
you leer at in unison.
All these fine bodies of men
of course before their first quart
believe that Capitalism
in its inevitable death-throes
is subjugating women
and list the times like conquests
they've been liberal to a tee.
Eddie, my old blind pigeon,
they talk a load of shite
I bet ya five to one
a straight tenner, late at night
among their unwashed breakfast plates
beneath their 'Che' posters
they take out funny pictures.
Those sweet, fantastic pictures, Eddie
all those eager beavers,
naughty, naughty photographs, Eddie
the kind their dying mummies
would slap their spotty bottoms
for ever even contemplating...

It's all in Nostradamus, kids

Even when borders close
when there are hourly bulletins
transmitted by radio hams
on crackly crystal sets
through sandbags & crossfire,
even when the chemical labs
are working flat out,
when the mounted politzei
waltz gaily through the market place,
when there are curfews,
riots in the supermarket,
tit for tat killings,
even on the night of the long knives
where, children, will we find Eddie?
You guessed it, junior,
have an apple from teacher
he'll still be in the basement
swopping drug tales with playmates,
the day the squad came in force
& cordoned off the entire area,
all the best places, kiddies
for all the secret stashes.
Yes, the same tired old patter, kids
all of them squatting like Indian Chiefs
& when they get the MUNCHIES
gobbling at satsumas
awaiting VEGE stew
sneering like hyenas
at contestants in the quiz show.
Let's do the fandango with Eddie, children
skip, skippity-skip
all the way to Armageddon.
Listen to him slabbering
'It's all in Nostradamus'
his hashish eyes luring
girls along the corridor,
his inane grin, all-embracing
as a limitless nuclear winter...

Sufferin Eddie

Eddie
that's a girl at the bus-stop
that's all
a girl at the bus-stop

She doesn't fancy you
for any reason
nor is she in the slightest bit
like Meryl Streep

She wasn't born & nurtured
to be bothered with you
sheep eyes!
She isn't a cover girl
nor is she a cindy doll
for your greasy little mitts

So scuttle along, Eddie
disappear
& take your wee action man...

The way of Eddie

So what's brought this sudden uplift, Eddie,
this space face & feeling of supreme well-being?
Are you laced up with Cough Mixture again?
Is this some new Designer Natural High?
& what's all this balls & baloney, Eddie
about Karma & the river's eternal flow?
D'ye take me for a complete Buck Eejit?
Purity comes easier to the devil, Eddie
You're the patron saint of Nervous Wrecks,
you're the Godfather of pervert sex
& cheap pornography.

16

So now you're in tune with the infinite,
in rhythm, Ed, with your aura & the spheres
'& every blade of Shitgrass is fantastic,
looks so majestic' I hear you pray,
'all moves with sychronicity & is divine,
see the bees guzzling down their pollen
& the bush in its joyous blossom.'

Sure you don't know the trees' names, Eddie
& birds to you are just cartoon furry friends.
Where's your *Observer Book of Plants*, Eddie?
What's this flower called then, eh?

Christ! You're an advert for a Lobotomy, Eddie
& ok the Way of Zen is an honourable path
but not for the like of you
with your liquid lunches & yellow tongue
you can't stand upright on this lino, Eddie,
never mind walk steadfast on the astral plane.
You can't negotiate the corner shop, Eddie
let alone the suffering of the Holy Grail.
You're about as mystical as a cabbage, Eddie
as enlightened as a dollop of cement.

Everytime I clock you, Eddie
I think, 'how profoundly sad
ah such fodder for my tears!'
'there's poor Eddie' I think
doesn't he strive & try hard
but with his face like Circusboy, old twister,
he's away with the mixer
poor Eddie's lights are always on
but there's never anyone in...

Meter readings

Eddie, if you have the fear
or a doze of the noia
or the crawling heebie-geebies
don't blame me

trace back in the infantry
count them all, Eddie
those you've slept with
since 1973

every blow-out
every quick blow-job, Eddie
it's time to have them analysed

suddenly there is bad blood
between us

& when you kissed
Miranda Churchill Londonderry Smith
in the bog end
of the bike shelter
did you have a mouth ulcer?

have you slipped the hand
round something rotten
once too often?

have you finally disposed of tenderness?
will there be true romance left
when you live in spooky quarantine?

have you any wits in store
to have about you, Eddie
when the radio spells it out
& you contort your furry face?

WELCOME PEOPLE TO THE FINISHING POST
PEOPLE OF THE HUMAN RACE...

Prayer for the barely standing

Such a hideous waste, Eddie
your illegal smile wearing thin
ashtrays & hubbly-bubbly pipes
haunting the smell of your deathbed
when you end up wired up to machines

tubes up your nose, Eddie
that'll spoil your cute kisser
charts & graphs on downward slopes
& your pickled lungs held aloft
as reminders to the lily-whites
the Big C, Eddie, discuss:

& your liver will be shredded too
cancelling all its devilry out
in a whirling dirvish of Special Brew

& you were never really at the ballgame
out to lunch you were never there
climbing the ornate wallhangings
still comotose in your chair

& on the barstool you preach on, Eddie
many wee blighters called tumours
have sprouted as you've speeled

so keep on playing the wurlitzer, Eddie
sing along with all the loony tunes
talk more gibberish to the optics
cos just for now your song plays on
as the old ticker disintegrates
& the scratchy needle scrapes
across the plastic of your hours

so you've learnt a few new songs, Eddie?
very good, how about a few?
how about 'ONE DAY AT A TIME, SWEET JESUS
THAT'S ALL I'M ASKING OF YOU'...

Return of Sensitive Eddie

Welcome back from the health farm, Eddie
you're looking well, are you sick?
after all that fresh air & herb tea
lay off the auld Clandew, Eddie
lay off the auld Scotsmac
or next month you'll just be back
propping up the wine bar altar
rambling & gambling & shambling, Eddie
your crooked wee eyes cocked
at any tight skirt in sight

Was not meditation blissful, Eddie?
was not brown rice beneficial?
so don't end up back in bedlam, Ed
up to your oxters in shite
no more wacky backy, stay steady, Eddie
keep your zipper in its clipper
no more pervy polaroids either
or horsing back the jungle juice
that sends you, Ed, all of a dither

SOBER
SOBRIETY
there, I've said it, Eddie
now that was fairly painless

Not a bit of wonder, Eddie
as in the good old fruity days
you're covering your ears with your paws
& sprawling about on the stormy sea
of your bed-settee-put-me-up
like Caligula on a bad day, Eddie

I hate to see you suffer like this, Ed,
here, have a blast of this...

Pooh-pooh

Sure we should have known
you'd be out of your dome
on solvents, Eddie, glue

is there no noble causes left
to catch a feeble grip of?

lighter fuel won't make you cool
if you ignite
its gentle barbarism
will trail you offstage early
blithering & babbling

& Evostik just drives you screwy, Ed
fierce stuff altogether the auld glue
you'll wander through this riot footage, Eddie
like a headless horse in a cartoon
like the legendary Mr Magoo
you'll glide blithely through the murders
through the gutted polling booths

& when it all goes dangerously askew
amid the sizzling barricades
in the heavy truncheon charge
there will only be hypermarkets, Eddie
belonging to zipperheads & sharks
& you'll end up hyperventilating
living in the doorway of Marks & Sparks

& your face will stick to lamp-posts, Eddie
its sticky gunge of tears
come out of this lustre
let me soothe your crazy fears
JUST SAY NO & crawl back to bed
why not wait for the state, Eddie
to kill you off instead...

Lounge lizards

Ok Eddie if you really insist
her name, my little milksop,
is Felicity Montague Python Smith
daughter to the wayward daughter
of the country squire

& I can't for the meagre life of me
for the meat, the murder or the life of me
work out what she's doing here!
this is Slumsville Ed, the pits
& his nibs in the manor would do his nut
if he saw her here scooping pints down
or firing back wee ones
amid these plastic flowers

STAY BACK, EDDIE
Down sniffer, down!
you horny wee gett, Eddie
quit gawking

it would serve you right, Eddie
if she hit you a smack in the bake
stop cruisin the distant highway
of her ragged crimson hair
stop tracing her shape in the air

she's out of your league, Eddie
the Python Smiths have servants
who have servants themselves, so there
she's not in your league, Edward
which looking at your belly
as you burp & inflate yourself
is the 4th division, Eddie
somewhere near the bottom end...

CRACK

Devils

& so we meet again
after tiffs & scuffles
in your pine kitchenette

Why is it, I wonder,
I feel only this urge,
this ridiculous urge
to re-arrange the atmosphere?
Think I'll smash up
all your poxy jam jars
crammed with rice & lentils,
with those woeful ADUKI beans

Later, like the speaking clock,
you'll still be prattling
down here oblivious in the debris,
while I'll be upstairs
muttering PROPERTY IS THEFT
in your lavish bathroom
or maybe upturning beds
hunting out Daddy's
pricless antique knick-knacks,
hurling them with glee
like paper planes,
aiming them straight
at your sensitive cats
with their pretentious names,
as they skulk in the yard
near the patio door...

Disneyland

We're just cruisin
through the afternoon
two cans of lager
& a spliff
on the roof

the police down below
on secret manoeuvres
don't frighten me!
may as well be pandas
frolicking
may as well be plastic men

quick!
Rodney, quick
skin up another one
don't want to miss
the destruction of daylight
at four o'clock...

Another encounter

What's she doing with that asshole,
I once said. Now she's sitting here with me.
We talk over separations, how much they cost.
I've frayed with years but she still clings
to delicacy. Her fragile wrist reaching for lager,
her raised arms speaking deliberate messages.
I notice how the bikers in the corner still want her.
It's plain from the grimace each wears on his face,
she's still in fashion. If I could read their lips
they'd mutter to each other in unkempt voices,
What's she doing with that asshole?

Drugs

Pleasure takes years
to perfect
a room draped
with Indian cloth,
the hearth that feeds
on Rizla scraps & ash.

One more hot knife
before you go stumbling
into the sodium glare
babbling aloud.

Grounds of Asylum

I've seen them often as I cross the lawn,
their dishevelled committee meeting
beneath drooping branches.
They sit on benches bestowed to them
by last century's gentlemen.
Strange, I should always notice
their white stubble, how short
they wear their cast-off trousers.
Murmuring, they always seem to stare
like nomads to an aimless distance.
Indeed from over here, in the new block
they could be mistaken for scarecrows
flapping their arms at pigeons.
I laugh when I see them on trains
or buses, disrupting clerks or shoppers,
ranting about Vikings.
Their grinning faces always make me
want my childhood back.

Home brew & video

Turns out
we could have made it
to the speedway after all,
but we just couldn't raise ourselves
once we'd settled down.
Completely lethal stuff!

I was scanning the papers
with malice,
next thing I know
she'd sprawled across me,
cuddled up!

I sneered
at right-wing bias
& she tittered,
rising as usual
to fiddle a bit
with the knobs...

Fallen Angels

Then gulping rum in a desperate sweat
my clothes strewn about me
the dream of our freehold dissolves.
Let's face it, Angel, we'll never connect.
Hawthorn will still blossom
but oblivious of us.
We who belong to chemicals & bedsits,
to these late-night bouts of self-destruction.

So accept you'll never cause a scandal
with outrageous skirts or hairdos,
never turn the heads of frustrated farmers
in the bars or chapels of the outback.

27

And I'll never rise with a clear head,
cycling through the autumn frost
to buy groceries at the crossroads.
What's more, our unborn children,
a whole fleet of them
with names like Klee or Ophelia,
will never run wild & undisciplined
trampling the vegetable rows
we'll never even try to nurture.

Scratchmarks

I've heard toothpaste
removes lovebites –
at least a salesman
I hitched from Knutsford
Services told me so,
& he drove a Volvo
with buttons to adjust
reclining seats
and headrests,
so who was I to doubt?

What I wanted to know, though
was what would happen
if his suspicious wife…
From what he told me
her passion was more for
double-layer cream cakes
than Charlie's flights of fancy,
what would happen if
returning albeit reluctantly
from some foreign trip
having secured orders
to secure in turn
new garage doors
new patio furniture
& Jason's ski trip,

if he, the wild rover,
had dirty great big
scratchmarks from some
thin Belgian hussy
on his spider–like back
or inside arm?

'Easy' he said
cruisin past juggernauts
like Steve McQueen,
'Easy...
I'd just say it was quiet
and all the men were desperate,
so competing for contracts
we wrestled a bit together...'

Newcastle is Benidorm

girls on Friday exit routes
in flimsy skirts & skimpy t shirts
all brandish castanets
& form a human party chain
to dance thru Eldon Square

with the skill & dexterity
of bullfighters depicted
on trinkets & souvenir ashtrays
the 'lads' in the bravado after hours
hover in doorways makin moves

& safe sex hasn't been invented
& all the bars tonight were hivin
& the sky's the colour of sun tan lotion
& I'd give a million to be so neutral
& everywhere has become a haze
of free offers & tabloid slogans
& disco rhythms insidious & thumping
& the crowd from the Pizza house jumping
into litter bins & pissin on windows

selling fridge freezers & community singing
& groping hands & fumbling tongues at bus stops
& football arguments & the ringing
of alarm bells set off for 'high jinks'
& the stale boke on the floor of the Bacchus tavern
& all down the cubicles in nightclubs – stinks
& there will never be an armed uprising
against the Capitalist Conspiracy here
or anywhere else for that matter –
what a crying shame!...

'Here we go, Here we go, Here we go'...

Creep

Judith was just 16
I was 43

what an endeavour
talking to her
about pop music
turned out to be

I'm a bit creepy

that's what I heard
her whispering
to her mates

'he's a bit creepy'...

Not Jack

Strange thing was
when his wife puked
up her bar meal
in the County Hotel
he didn't take even
a blind bit of notice.

It seems the girl
on the telex machine
in the executive suite,
she of the clinging skirts,
had pointed out last week
his slight resemblance,
only slight mind you,
to Jack Nicholson.
So it was this
and only this
on his mind right now.

He just kept glimpsing
like a monkey
glimpsing through the mirror
as though afraid
he'd vanish,
kept flicking back
his greasy hair,
behind his shades
he was hiding
from the masquerade.

Like a jelly with
whipped cream
she wobbled, belched
blubbered & spat
but he just went on
studying the optics,
the array of spirit bottles.

You'd swear he'd been
snorting powder!
Just kept wishing
this was Sunset Boulevard
and he wasn't plain Harry
but fast Jack.

'Hey Baby' he said
as her face appeared up
smudged with tomato sauce
& succulent french fries
the waiters sprinting about
in manic disarray
'Hey Baby
you wanna nother shot
we've got something goin babe
you wanna nother shot...'

How cynical the postcards were

you sent from Europe's youth hostel,
those gaudy prints from shops
selling the non-materialist life.

you probably scribbled them
over roll-ups & mocca
in seedy, oh famously seedy cafés
or perhaps you penned them
on some worn municipal bench
in the park where rucksacks of 11 nations
basked together in sunshine
as their owners deliberated maybe
over hidden meanings in Kafka
& kept their journals bubbling over
beneath the hashish sky

it wasn't always this way, surely?
may I venture to surmise
you've been delving too deeply
into the book on EXISTENTIALISM
I lent you in 1973?

I can recall your innocence
recall for instance, the MONET reproduction
you sent when museums still 'amazed' you
remember the side with the exotic stamp
smothered in hugs & kisses
the message devoid of irony:
'you have brought harmony
& balance & good vibes
back into my heart
I love you like a plateful
of my favourite marshmallows
like the lambskin sweater
my mummy bought me
a long long time ago'...

What to do on a wet Wednesday

That's the snooker off now
till 5 past 7 on BBC 2
so what's it to be?

ok Abbott & Costello
at 5.15 but until then?

whow!
I've grown another two fingers!
that car cruisin the multi-storey
looks just like Thunderbird 3
everyone, including me,
looks as I envisaged
people on Venus would look
all GOOGLE-EYED...

I sometimes wish I really was
an alien instead

no giro yet
& the rustle & bustle of rain
falling like mercury

oh, how science, the Bible
& the Beano fit into perspective
when you're an empty vessel

suppose I could have another cup of tea
& stitch my Oxfam raincoat

THIS IS EARTH, THIS IS DEFINITELY EARTH
I've convinced myself of that much...

Tiffin

Simply everyone was there
the crème de menthe
of the county

I could barely speak
for all the garlic mushrooms
they were cramming deliriously
into my cake hole

it was a riot
it was a hoot

the Muscat 82 I mean
I horsed it down me
like a dose of Ribena

& as for the bathroom
don't talk to me about the bathroom
the bathroom was about the size
of Hampden Park

I finished up
somewhere near the penalty spot
spewing up my guts
seeing 'Ralph & Hughie'
to the sound of roaring

'hurrah hurrah hurrah'
drifting up from downstairs...

Crack

It was a piece of piss then
I'd cracked it

& when the foamy coffees came
we showed off old photographs
from our old bus passes

her freckles, my black rings

& as the woman wiped the floor
we raised our feet in unison
& I knew then that I'd cracked it
when she twiddled her ringlet
dipped her wide saucer eyes
& spoke those magic words

'So what star sign are you then?'

Life's a long song

Look it might sound hard
but don't mention the bastard

if it wasn't for Freud
I'd be gainfully employed

& I wouldn't be moribund
if it wasn't for Sigmund

he's turned us into nervous wrecks
speeling on about sex

morning noon & night
the same old gobshite

do I fancy my brother?
do I fancy my mother?

incest! penis envy! all SEX
– me with no job or prospects

reckon he takes me for a sucker
should have knifed him

the arrogant wee fucker...

Pastoral

look at all these sheep
stuffin' their bakes with grass
I hate the open spaces!

where's the concrete?
where's the chemicals?

someone in this outback
must have a TV

& I desperately need
a juicy STARBURGER
with double french fries

hey farmer joe
rustic face
which way to the motorway?

no I don't want
to see your fucking goats...

Crap

I'm really sorry Matilda
but your party was crap

I couldn't summon the energy up
to spew up or abuse the stupid people

I never had a Marxist rant
when I'm not fired up I can't

I drank in the lounge of lethargy
burnt out Bertie with no sap

no harm to you Matilda
but your party was crap

waltzing Matilda waltzing Matilda
who'll come a waltzing Matilda

with me...

The exchange visit

Well I woke up this morning
& I was in Czechoslovakia
a peaceful suburb of Prague
to be exact

it had rained
so the lawns all glittered
& I had a splitting head
from too much 80% vodka
well presumably so –

the whole thing is a mystery
because now I talk the language
I have a Czech wife
three handsome healthy Czech children
(for the moment their names escape me)
a Czech house with a Czech roof
overlooking a Czech swimming pool

what luxury!

it's really quite some existence
I've carved out for myself
& I've read Kafka in the original
& all my old favourites like Philip Marlowe
in handy pocket-sized Czech translations

still I have a job remembering
how I fell asleep
beneath the shadow
of the lame cow
at the edge of Mulligan's field
in the drizzle
in the breezes whirling tractor blades
in the old sod

yes I have a job recollecting
how I woke like this hungover
in this suburb of Prague

which thankfully is very handy
to all of the shops

what utter luxury!

Kylie, be mine

I celebrated down the pub
upon joining your Fan Club

there's such wildfire & magic
in all your supreme machinery

Kylie, it's profoundly tragic
you'll never cuddle up to me

I want you like tasty Chop Suey
your dance steps send me all guey

& it never seems like hard labour
when you 'take it to the top'

my sugar pig, adorable neighbour
don't ever ever stop

Kylie, your face soothes my fears
you touch me in places

I've touched myself in for years...

Swing

'the bare-faced audacity
some fucking cheek!'

my wife,
scarlet-faced
clattered down the salad bowl
hard on the pine bench

I was spreading honey
the length of my Waffles
some would say mellow
as the still pond

she was foaming at the mouth
'unreal' I thought

we haven't made love for 13 years
so I brought home my girlfriend
it seems in a moment of forgetfulness
she started wearing my wife's suit
& some of her more intimate
knick-knacks as well
went astray

my girlfriend is called Astril
she's good fun

not like my wife
though I like her
I suppose

It's a strange set up I muse
sort of Bohemian
as with juice on my tongue
I decide in a flash

think I'll spend the rest of the day
flaked out

on the hammock...

Pooper

I am shit-faced
by the time I arrive, paralytic

I can barely walk even
by the time I drive home

& everyone always looks the same
or worse still like Policemen

& someone usually finds me in a garden
babbling, sometimes of rapture

oh, I wish I could levitate
it would make thinking less awesome

so leavin late & steamin
I mouth to people in ridiculous jumpers

'sorry, gotta go, run out of platitudes'...

To Sir With Love

that corduroy jacket
will have to go

so what if it cost a packet
the image just doesn't fit

& those meaningful stares
are no longer a hit

the girls are getting younger
perhaps it's time you quit

listen to Tracy on the noon-day bus
'I hate Geography

it's fuckin shit'...

Confession

True, I'm a volatile man,
constantly on a spring & fiery

the sort who subconsciously
really wants you all to read my diary

get the juice on the drugs, the sex,
savour the majestic flavour of my wordplay

even if I had vicious acne, wore milk-bottle specs
you just wouldn't be able to stay away

if I had garlic breath constantly, my feet always smelt,
still into my beefy arms you'd melt

were I Lucifer, big Uncle Satan himself,
I'd never fear being left on the shelf

which makes me feel better, basking in the fame
so every morning to the whiskey mirror

I repeat it: 'Hello again, whatshisname'…

Are you lonesome tonight?

this bar's too fuckin bright!
the mood! the atmosphere's not right!

you used to touch just about anything
& it would become adorable

now I'm drunk & want to give you a ring
& when I drink, as you know, I'm deplorable

when I drink I want to go back
just back, anywhere! after a stack

of pints, rums, tequila slammers I'm reeling
these charades make me wonder if feeling

is just what happens on the TV
– the only thing that helps is my bed

& I could phone you now it's way past 3
you might say: 'Christ, thought someone was dead

I might say: 'no, worse than that, it's me'…

Peter Pan on acid

Girls! I'm the maestro you just won't believe
I guarantee you'll leave my flat much less naive,

more schooled, learned, shall we say. There's my books
old Rockabilly tapes, my profound lingering looks

& you don't know what you've missed
if you haven't yet been kissed

by someone with my wisdom & sensitivity.
come on up! I'll make us both a herbal tea,

sure I'm never without a stack of dope
& some vague talk of astrology

my I Ching & Beefheart albums offer hope
that you'll snuggle like teddies up to me

there was a time when I got excited, free & bold,
but that was long ago when you were only 3

before you were even young & I was even old...

Harpers & Queen & Steve

Beautiful people are always late
if they bother to turn up at all

I crane my neck in foyers
in queues they scorn

glimpse their dimples
& wallet's thickness

when they beckon like Emperors
for ice & bubbly cocktails

they may as well be asking
'fetch me essence of the wind'

as I swallow my bitter apple
cough twitch stammer & jerk

think 'I will bring you Anything
my flowers of the vale if you press me'

oh how I wish the beautiful people would
press me that is...

Friend

I miss your wreckage
in my flat

clothes thrown down
& lipsticks

everything's neat again
back in order
& I think that's shameful
don't you?

chaos was my friend

Transylvania
(for Kathryn)

1 *Transylvania*

I've been hanging out down at the station again
since you left for Paris. Grim! Christopher Lee!

That's how bad it is. People can all see my sickness,
women run quickly into shops when they see my face.

I'm Dracula again looking for victims on platform 3,
eyeing the beauties in the bustle, in the tannoy haze.

Look! here they come now with their tube bags.
Watch me suck them dry! Listen to my invitation!

'Roll with me beauties off the edge of your lives'
Nightmare. That's the only word for a date with me

& that buffet girl's not interested, it's plain to see,
'it's the Spook,' she thinks, 'the Vampire of platform 3'

'it's the man with the pencilled-in hairline! quick!
it's Christopher Lee! he's creepy & hairy, garlic!'

So there you have it, grim isn't it, Christopher Lee,
that's me, hanging out at the station since you left

looking for blood, blood to forget you for a while,
blood to be back home since we've been apart,

home in a box in Transylvania with the stakes beside my heart...

2 *Revolution*

It's turn of the century Russia, ok?
you're a Countess & I'm a serf.

Get the picture, a bogman with a scythe,
out chopping fields with scythe for your heart

knowing it's hopeless as the winter stings.
Up in Petrograd you'll be getting restless

in the snow, beside your bourgeois fire & maids
who heat up all your muffs, help keep your feelings

buried, subdued by the palace, its majestic food,
the grandeur of a thousand dinner parties

to obscure me, to obscure you from my face
that night in the lonely carriage, a samovar

on the low light later in my shack, my bogland.
So Peter will be telling me soon of revolution

& then we'll have to fight, my dear, on different sides.
Your world will be turned upside-down, my darling

& my voice will ache calling out to the hinterland
before the begining of the end, the dust of our love

trampled as the citizens storm the barricades.
You won't ever escape me in exile either,

on the meadow beside the Finnish lake so still…

3 *Rot*

There's dry rot in the attic, sweetest, & we never speak,
how are we supposed to sort out this rot then?

There's dust everywhere & now in the attic this rot,
we need treatment, sweetest, we need to see an expert.

If only we could see the village handyman even,
but he's out of town, poor simpleton, riding away

over the hills on his bike with a lucky sixpence
was the last heard of that fella, no handyman!

No expert! So we've got big problems here, my sweet,
& I'm no good with rot, I can grow things no problem,

look at the hyacinths I planted sure, their radiance!
but DIY? you may as well whistle something backwards!

Who can lend us the readies, sweet, the dosh, the LSD?
surely not the bank manager, my sweet, a lost cause.

He's out on the green right now with his new putter
& dry rot's the last thing he ever thinks about,

not ours, not his, not anybody else's. No bankman can save us.
No money from the moneyman can save our dry rot.

Have you even been up to the attic of late, my sweet?
remember love beneath the candles, giggling at the beams?

no, I don't suppose you've been up there of late, my sweet,
it's a wreck, devastation! not the dream home we seek.

our attic is caving in, my sweet, & we never speak...

4 *Bye bye love*

I'm packing my heart off to boarding school,
it just has to be done, I can't control it.

Perhaps the stern brothers & nuns can help
knock some degree of discipline into my heart.

A cold shower at 5 in the morning, a 6 mile run
through the mud & the mire, some meditation.

Let my heart learn prayers for being so crazy!
Let my heart scrub floors for penance!

Discipline! Bed with no malted milk! No sugar!
Not a spoonful of sugar will my heart be given,

& I won't even send my heart a care package.
No care packages, I'm running my heart out of town.

You big softie, heart, you snivelling wee weasel!
Save all your tears & snotters for the nuns.

Now I'll get to invite the neighbour in for champagne.
I'll seduce the neighbour's wife effortlessly.

I'll seduce the neighbour's mistress heartlessly
while the neighbour groans & drinks my poison tea

& my heart by then will have forgotten me...

5 *Black ice*

It's like there's been this massive car crash
& our love has wrapped itself round a tree,

or we've toppled over completely on the hard shoulder,
the tyres of strangers squirting us as they speed by.

Mud & slime from puddles in our hearts on the M6,
let's make it the M6, our love in heavy fog.

So we should have gone by the B roads, my love,
should have travelled by all the scenic routes,

stopped for pints, stopped for plenty of bacon buns,
smoked over tea & breakfasts in all the wild domains.

But how we rush, we always rush & now we're comotose
& the ambulance won't come, we've had our 15 minutes,

& that AA man is surely kind but what can we do?
the dents on the bodywork like an earthquake's hit,

the steering wheel all bent & petrol leaking.
So we lie half-dead with our half-remembered prayers

& that kind AA man can do nought, my love & no doctors either
will just be happening along on their way to conventions.

It won't be like the movies now, my dearest, not now,
because our love is wrapped around the steel barrier

& our blood is running thin, we're slipping away, my love,
to some burnt out scrapyard, it's a migration upwards,

up to Jesus with his roadmap & his pencil poised
to seal our fate. 'Pick a place, Jesus,' he thought;

'Where can I find the place to take back their souls?'
Aye, we're in deep water now, my dear, banjacksed,

up shit river with no paddle, up the grim M6,
& that home in the hills we promised ourselves, my dear,

is just over the rise if we could only make it, if fuel
could be found or the ambulance did come miraculously.

'Look! here comes the ambulance men with their gleaming faces'
I'll utter, our hands stretching out to each other

in the mess & in the fractured air...

6 *Mona*

I'm living in this attic now with my new girlfriend,
does that make you jealous? do you envy her?, my Mona.

Her name's Mona, the bright elusive butterfly of love,
& I've packed in whiskey, the breath of Satan, since we met.

At night when I'm sad it's good to hear her fluttering
& she hangs out on my windowledge in the slow afternoon.

She preens herself endlessly & although she flaps in panic
I wouldn't harm her, Mona's safe with me, I swear it!

You mustn't think I wouldn't let her float away either,
I let you float away, remember, the streets beyond our nest.

A friendly neighbour is keeping our nest spick & span
& look, I realise if we go back there it's without her.

But you'd like her, she's an orange shade I warm to,
Mona's looking after me in her own wild mystical way.

Together we look through your photos & she soothes me,
beautiful Mona's my latest but you'll never be my ex.

One day we'll be back in that nest together, I know it!
you can kick over as many cups of tea as you like,

you can watch TV & ask dumb questions endlessly all night,
you can get me to fetch hot pitta breads & peanut butter,

I'll fetch the croissants too & the durex bill is mine,
& all the days just lying about in our nest will be precious.

Mona understands all this, don't fret, it's just a phase,
another phase we're going through, Mona & myself agree

she'll fly one day beyond the factories, set us both free...

THE IRISH CARD

Brian's Fables

How come I'm starting to feel more distant, like a pop star,
when I meet up with the old Eagles team in The Whitecliff?

They can remember all my antics on the pitch better
than I can. 'Arthur, you're a fuckin onion' I shouted

because he was useless & that time I took my shirt off
& handed it to the psycho full-back saying 'here, have it',

when he fouled me & the day there was a minute's silence
for some league official so the Ref blew his whistle

& the Prof went steamin down the wing shouting for the ball,
he had to walk back feeling a right eejit & we cracked up

& there was that game on a cow field at the back of Carnlough,
Fat screaming at the specky Ref who didn't book him, no way,

didn't send him off either, just ripped out the corner flag,
ran at him & threatened to 'carry his fuckin head off!'

& I had to be called Brian when we played away fixtures,
at least in some places, say in Ballyclare where the Dirts

in their bomber jackets waved Red Hands & Union Jacks
behind the goalposts weren't anything abnormal & fights

were many & games got abandoned & once the old Whitehead team
had to leap in their cars, escape with their kit still on.

Brian has stuck with me since. I've always needed an alias
& all this floods back to me as I dander about, & steamin

someone like D.J. rolls over, grips my arm & asks me:
'Boutya Brian, how long are ye home for?'

& I think 'more like how long before I get away!'...

Wedding in Omagh

'Am I an alien or what?' I wondered
at that July wedding somewhere near Omagh.

The night before a wake was happening too
so a steady stream of punters came to the parlour

& Maggie's aunt wore a man's coat, smoked Old Holborn
& boiled her uncle's eggs in a rusty old peach tin.

No kidding! when she got the ham sandwiches out
they came from a drawer in the sideboard,

no plates & all of this watched over by the bride's mother,
she'd become a vegetable through giving birth

& you couldn't tell as she rocked in her chair
making wailing sounds, if she disapproved of anything

or everything was turning out as she hoped.
& I knew how far I'd wandered when revellers teased Thomas,

the bridegroom, rolling their eyes, nudging him about the honeymoon
& I honestly got the feeling they'd not fucked yet

& all that innocence puts a strain on me & at the wedding
the priest picked out members of the crowd, taunting

'Take stock of this, Mick, it could be your turn next'
or 'Pat, I see you've the best suit on for the ladies'.

After the reception, muddled about my future, & whiskey
lapping round my stomach, I caught the Belfast bus

then the next day the ferry to Stranraer's ugliness.
In my head I could hear my mother speaking:

'Aye, son, you'll learn, far away fields are green'...

Brighton

'Don't look at me, I didn't plant it'
would be what I'd say if they heard me

ordering 'Vodka & White' or Guinness 'by the neck',
my voice bellowing in the wrong place as usual

& surely they should know a buddy like me
would hardly have done it. I'm too loafish,

my politics are soft. I'm the student type,
arty as fuck, not the bomber type at all.

But they just can't keep themselves from believing
'Aye, he says this & he says that but what do we know?

I'd say there was more te that fella than meets the eye!'
Well there isn't. I just want to get by quietly

& although my friends in the party lament it,
that they didn't get Thatcher, I have to disagree.

It's not of course because I don't hate her,
but imagine it, the machinery of witch hunts!

I'm already half-convinced my phone's tapped
& then that break-in I had, well who really knows?

Nothing was taken but maybe someone, some spy
wasn't removing things but putting them in!

get my drift, bugging devices! I mention Brighton
& my voice is recorded. They know me from computers.

I used to go to Brighton too, day trips with Maggie.
'It's like London at the seaside' I always said,

'too much for a poor old country boy like me'...

The reunion

Tim, Spierre & myself now all finally agree
the insidious wee shithole has marked us.

We grew up surrounded by people dropping acid
in Ma Hambo's cafe, wishing we belonged to 'the scene'.

Derm & Pip in a weird sort of way were heroes
but now they're not. We see them as they are

& I'm thankful for that & the cannabis myth I lived in
for years in Teesside, days blotted out, wasted,

& my paranoia years in London squats were wasted too.
Tim is getting balder & Spierre wants some affection.

He says he gets none & hasn't had a cuddle let alone sex
for nearly a year & sure we all fancy younger women.

Instead of reading *The Way of Zen* back then, quoting the *I Ching*
we should have been sticking it up a load of wee girls!

& Christ! when I think of Anne McDonald! what an asshole!
she wanted a jump! but I just kept on spouting poetry,

& Spierre calls this state 'a deep sense of profound longing'
as at the window we drool out like dirty old men

getting brainless, accepting there's no miracle cure.
But that wee shithole in Ireland has marked us,

there's no doubt at all on that score...

Nights at the Irish Club

It's become so fashionable for me now
to attend the sessions down the Irish Club.

Amongst the old exiles transported by aires
I too wish I had some gaelic to speak of,

wish all the travel brochure posters on the walls
were the glamourous homeland I knew.

I horse back 10 or 11 pints of Murphys
& wait for the reels to spin me back,

back to the idyllic hearths & cottages,
to a green mosaic of good-natured decency,

to the barren cliffs & glens that haunt me
only when I pretend to strangers that I miss them.

Gerry on the fiddle hasn't been back since the war,
he wears a plastic shamrock & scans *Ireland's Own*.

He still gets some soda farls sent like me
but that's as far as it goes I'm afraid.

I'm a bona fide émigré turned far too cynical
to scoop the green beer on Patrick's Day,

to go on a spree & stand for the Soldier's Song,
to stumble out of here wishing myself in 'God's Land'.

As it is here anyway there are constant reminders,
the man with the shard-glass voice drunk up the entry

mouthing the Sash as he pisses & sways...

Safe to say

I was never asked it when I should have been,
say in dodgy bars hivin with UVF men.

Gangs of marauding tartan hoods never taunted me,
never forced me to pray up back entries,

never pulled flick knives asking for my alphabet,
upon hearing my 'h' sticking me with blades.

No – it seems I never had to prove myself either way
till I came to this country of patronising smiles.

English people with no malice ask me all the time,
their puzzled faces in the bloom of ignorance

– the sort of ignorance I'd call conspicuous,
the sort we are all really dying from.

'So are you a Catholic or Protestant then
if you don't mind me asking that is?'

It slips into idle chatter like the weather
& yes I do mind you asking I want to tell them

but I don't, so I usually make a joke of it,
with blood watered-down I stare at neutral glances.

Seeing no traits of instinct, or recognition
I say 'now take a good hard look there, Chappies,

sure the Pope shines out of my eyes'...

Rose

There was my ideal girl even way back then
at Carrick Grammar & I knew I'd find her 'across the water'.

You see, that's seen as a logical step & entirely natural
to go via Liverpool or Stranraer to colleges & careers

over on the mainland & that was where I knew she was.
For the want of a better name let's call her Rose,

I thought she might live somewhere like Hampshire
& she would have horses & speak with marlies in her bake,

but I wouldn't mind because of her beauty & lustre,
no way, not after growing up with a stack of wee Millies,

girls in Skinners & Crombies always shouting over
'Hey mister, my mate fancies ye' or 'mister, gotta feg?'

Rose would be refined & schooled, we'd discuss all the books
I longed to read, those I've never quite got round to

& one day I would have to go to her house like Bertie Wooster,
to her luxurious country estate where her pompous father

would want to know about my people & she'd be the pride
of all Hampshire but I'd charm her. I do it all the time,

lower my voice an octave & use load of quaint slang
& they love it & if I was a bastard it would get me laid & has done.

The Home Counties can't ever comprehend me, I'm an outsider,
it's a privilege to watch their class system in action

& I'm never thought of as pig ignorant, a bogman, but clever,
not like Macalpine's men or pissheads from Kilburn.

So Rose would be bowled over by my crack & lilting;
it would all be unreal to her, but enchanting. 'Talk about home,

it must be *so* romantic, is it really beautiful?' she'd ask me
& if I burped or let off a stinker after dinner, she'd tap me,

pretend to be disgusted, but I'd come off with some quip,
some cliché like 'Aye, sure ye can take the man out of the bog

but not the bog out of the man' & she'd be hooked again.
Needless to say this never happened & I never met her

no matter where I am nothing happens & I never meet her...

Sealink

I've left on this dreary boat once too often
so now this return route means home.

It doesn't mean Whitehead, its sloth & inelegance
or the blood & semen stirring Belfast bars.

Nor do I look back when I walk the plank
or stare transfixed from decks at dwindling docks.

There's nothing vaguely romantic to leave behind,
just the graffiti sprawl of miserable Larne,

the ignoble funnels & towers of Ballylumford
merging with the smog as my childhood slips.

Let's face it, I came here to escape bad blood,
a land of martyrs with their kneecaps smashed,

bonfires blaring as the war drums sound,
a debris of legs scooped into bin liners

& I wanted to escape the daggers behind language,
the subtle testing out process at teenage discos.

'What school do you go to then?' meant
'Which foot do you kick with? right or left?'

How you said it, Derry or the other place
registered a sharp & knowing smile.

I settle quick, hold back a flood of playbacks,
contemplating only breakfast I gaze straight ahead,

never even wipe back the window's condensation...

Well

For years my old bedroom stayed exactly as it had been,
the posters & the red bulb I seduced Louise under,

sprawled out on the floor perving to Santana,
beer mats from my first English trip on the wall

& stashed in the corner my old diaries from 74 & 75,
letters from girls I met on motorways, the infamous trip

Tim & I made to Dingle, loads of pints in O'Flaherty's bar
& when we got back he just couldn't hack it, coming down.

He tried to do himself in with a stack of Barbs & Roches
Mose had swiped from some chemical warehouse up in town,

leaving a note for his folks, ol' Pam & Eddie, under a brick
at the building site, he split off to Blackhead & the cliffs

completely deranged with the idea of growing up at all.
But unlike Steven Doggett he wised up just in time,

had his stomach pumped & learnt a huge lesson about contentment
like I did the day I realised that every time I come here

only emphasises how far it is I've strayed.
& it will always be hard to account for subtle changes

or explain how I live to my mother. She painted the room
8 years ago now, accepted I'd gone, lived now with Margaret,

that I wasn't on the verge of dropping things & returning,
exept for a few days, half from duty & then to linger

& pace through the old rooms in emptiness, in mute sunshine,
think about my father, can he still see me? how things had been.

How can I ever tell her truthfully the directions I've gone,
the seedy occasions, because there were some, the heartache

I discovered just didn't happen in the Hermann Hesse novels I read,
the blow, & all those ferocious sessions in TheThree Bulls Heads

or some patchouli attic a fleshy girl invited me to at 4 a.m.
after a feed of Brandy or Gin or somebody's Duty Free.

Tim is better. He's well. I'm well & if Louise came to visit
I'd probably crack & want to seduce her even now.

I think Santana are crap & have tossed down many beermats
onto the floor dejected since. My mother, thank Christ is well.

I sit in the kitchen mulling over papers & tell her
how much I paid for my new clothes & short hair & how I don't

eat fries now & we discuss my brother who is also well
& I've become conscious of the need to avoid making it seem

like I'm using her house like a convenient hotel...

On the border

One minute I'm idle, glimpsing fields & cattle,
scanning drab scenery the English would gloat over

next I see neutral clouds spread their blemish,
a chopper gradually swirling into view.

I suddenly start to probe bushes for camouflage,
envisage eyes from secret cameras clocking me,

sweat on my pale hands, then to make matters worse
we're flagged down by a jeep, rows of guns.

I can barely make out a nervous youngster's face
peering out from sandbags in the border pill box.

Each day he learns to live with shits & shivers,
the near-certainty of snipers' bullets – they harden to it

– they grow arrogant as the censor ersing History
substituting a very British form of truth.

Take for instance this cheeky cockney on the bus,
eyeing up bags on racks, beneath the seats.

Training his stare on my shaking face
contempt spreads as when he thinks of vomit.

He seizes up mutiny in our faces & I witness hate
– if I had the guts, which I don't, I'd spit

consider fields & cattle worth prison, or fighting for...

World View

I don't claim to come from anyplace, ideally speaking
I'm a World Citizen, sure saying so has got me in shtuck.

At Stranraer when the plain clothes boys stopped me,
turning out my pockets but I was clean & they were empty

& they asked me if I smoked & rifled through my roll-ups;
one cheeky fucker lifted my dreadlocks up, made snide comments.

So when they asked me on their forms if I was Irish or British,
I answered 'World Citizen' & they threatened to strip me

& they hoked through the 3 cases I was trailing home from Saltburn.
'An unemployed World Citizen, you're some boy', one joker taunted

& in the carpark later my mother was disgusted as still half-cut
from the clatter of pints on the ferry, I raised my voice, excited,

'Someone has to stand up & be counted', but I never did, nor will I,
& my mother said 'aye, you're a big boy now & know it all'

I suppose I thought I did but now I don't. I'm ignorant...

Down South

The day Derm drove me down south was a hoot,
smashed out of our brains on bump roads

& him pretending to be some heavy Ulsterman
complaining about potholes & Galtee cheese,

creeping Jesus statues everywhere in sight.
It had been sunny in Belfast but by the border

on the incline of a hill he poked me,
'There it is!' he said, 'the grey mist!'

'Why forsake the blue skies of Ulster
for the grey mists of the Irish Republic?'

We'd been pulled in & frisked in Armagh
& Ed Koch was in town, propegangering.

At the cathedral Derm used his wide-angle lens,
held high over the top of preying pressmen.

I've seen the snap since, Ed looks worried,
the way anyone would considering gunmen.

A Bishop was swanning about & this priest
I'd asked directions from pointed him out –

'That's the most powerful clergyman in Ireland!'
so Derm fiddled with his bag, whipped out his camera,

said 'He must be worth a shot, d'ye reckon?'
& that priest looked just like Ed had, alarmed

at how easy it would be & though helicopters
would probably spot ye, you could drain the breath

from anyone, just like that! So they pulled us, RUC, job,
but we weren't the hurtful kind, they knew it, just tourists.

I feel like that amid all the roadsigns in gaelic
& I'm not surprised after he dropped me off

Derm got more grief from a patrol over the border
& Bernard my host leaned over to me in 'The Black Kesh',

asked me how long I'd lived in England for
& when I told him, out of mischief he added

'thought there was a trace of West Brit in yer accent'...

Ulster: A Tourist Guide

Now when I return less with the latest gadgets,
with more than a sliver of saxon on my tongue,

I feel conspicuous like a tourist or being a 'trendy leftie'
I become a crack reporter on an undercover exposé.

My judgements click together now in newsreel,
the TV map of Belfast glowing, hangs on my brain

& because I'm an alien now & usually stoned & rootless
all the bombs & guns & bible thumping scare me more.

Men I grew amongst, who never caught the ferry out,
on my casual strolls hold sten guns to my throat.

As a child I'd practise jumping hedges with cars in pursuit,
now it's no joke, I may have to take a frantic leap

& the roadblocks leave me shuddering as my new friends would,
all my drinking cronies in the gardens of English pubs.

Let's just say one wants to take his 'wife & kid' over,
he's heard me often recommend the crack, the drink, the fishing

& I would have reassured him once, strenuously too,
told him to 'go for it', not to bother changing number plates,

told him to get wired into the authentic bars I immortalise,
told him sure you could get a bullet in the head anywhere.

Let's just say I used to say that, confident & relaxed,
but having lived here, a stereotype, for nigh on 12 years

I have to admit, though it hurts, now I'm not too sure...

Travels in the Motherland

The same scenario when I hitchhike
for nigh on 14 years now,

always salesmen with charged batteries
who hum, hum then talk incessantly

about their car, their wife's car,
potential threats to the no claims bonus.

They screech predictably to a halt
as the window slowly unwinds itself.

I'm usually thirsty, dust in my head,
coming or going reluctantly.

My automatic smile erupts
gathering its own stupid impetus

until they hear my Irish voice
cut their tyres like slashmarks.

Each as casual, original, they gulp:
'hope you haven't a bomb in the bag, Son'

I toss away my fag, watch it whirl backwards
on the slipstream of speed & gravel.

I ease my legs up against the dashboard,
relax as though I were riding shotgun.

'Hope you've no plastic bullets beneath the seat'
I quip, grin & yawn

a bit more...

Prodigal

All my old friends are becoming drug fiends
riding late at night to each other's houses

trying to score. Sure nothing's changed since the 70s
& apart from the advent of their new designer gear

the die-hard Loyalists haven't changed much either.
They used to give ye the nod all year round

but on the eleventh night fix you with a glare
that said 'on yer bike ye Papish Cunt!'

I can still see them creeping out at dawn
to paint 'Taigs Out' on the chapel steps

or guzzling Harp down in the promenade shelter
as they did in 72 screeching 'No Surrender'

all of them at the vanguard of a dream gone wrong.
My friends off course & bleary-eyed don't notice,

well that's not true, they just try & avoid it
as much as humanly possible. They cultivate

their allotments, 'Antrim Gold' they call it,
listen to Miles Davis, talk of consignments

late into the hours when seagulls swoop the railings
coming in to take all our thoughts away

& the crack in the bar gets worse, no escaping it,
this was home once but now it's like the film version.

I'm undesirable & always fluff my lines...

The Great Getaway

Back for Reading Week or Christmas I'd relocate myself,
nod to the odd stray face from school or teenage parties,

wonder if, in the bar's fickle air, they'd remember me,
if they can remember what it is I've strayed away from,

what it is I seek to steal from their fattening faces,
from the intrigue & adventures of their past without me?

Now I don't bother to try – here's another hip generation,
people I thought would always be 10 pissed in my place

& the cliffs at Blackhead, as they brood, no longer absorb me,
the revolving prisms of the lighthouse don't cage me

& the Marine Bar just reminds me of middle age arriving,
the local legends still holding court but looking jaded,

& as for me, well I'm the trendy guy in the London jacket
who flits in now & then to patronise & smirk.

I feel more inclined to speak with other emigrés
home like myself to appease their foreign mothers.

We drown out the drone of Ulster blood with chatter
discuss 'Thatcher', the desperate plight of Labour.

We may as well be in the Real Ale Lounge back yonder
with our filmscript of Ireland, our mythologies unravelling.

But this is the real thing & what I hear from the corner
where the locals sit, I suddenly have some sympathy for

'wish all these fucking students would go back'...

Slouch

Their bar-stools have slouched them too early
though later half-cut they start to sidle up

'Hey Pat, why not fuck off where you came,
back to the bogs, shouldn't you be picking spuds?'

They have eyes with no causes, their smug voices
in drunken unison jeer & mock my voice.

Perhaps when the hangover hits I'll take them up,
return meekly, submerge myself in landscape,

more like submerge myself in Black Bush –
bury myself in selfish small-town intrigue,

or if I had any passion left for bland slogans
I could even do my bit for the 'armed struggle'.

But the echo of Lambegs burst my skull,
I've spent too long licking up to England.

I've been the brunt of their stunted comedians
I've lived in comfort but amid canned laughter

& this latest encounter could come to fisticuffs
although till now I've played the Irish card with charm.

They probe me: 'Mick, do you even belong in this country?'
I won't slouch too early so I gleefully reply

'just as much as you belong in mine'...

Beer & sympathy

Just look at how their eyes all bulge
& they shake their heads in disbelief

when I tell them about the Romper Room,
informants battered with baseball bats

or the law of the paramilitaries on estates,
joyriders getting kneecap jobs & dealers

taken out & hooded & Black 'n' Decker drills.
Not, of course, that I've had direct experience.

I tell them 'Look, it's not like walking
out yer door having to dodge bullets,

it's the ghettos! You get a spooky sense something's
going on in the background. War's a condition of mind.

I just go, like yer average punter, about my business,
nothing happens, where I come from nothing happens much at all!'

& they get animated when I give them the crack about Tommy
driving his drugs van to chemists all over the province.

He was speeding, so this patrol of Brits pulled him at Crossmaglen –
'Listen mate, I'm a Prod round here, I'm not hangin about'

So they wanted to know what he was carrying & he said Heroin
& the squaddie gave him a big cheesy grin & confided

'we get a bit of acid ourselves now & then.' Imagine it!
Lying in a ditch at the border tripping out all night!

Apocalypse Now wouldn't be in it! & the roadblocks are heavy,
at checkpoints it takes a soldier about 30 seconds

to suss you out on his walkie-talkie. See up in Lisburn
there's this massive computer & the heap of us are on it.

Sure, they've been using this place as a training ground
& in *Low Intensity Operations* Commander Kitson spells it out.

They know how to distort all ye see on yer tellies
& sure, plastic bullets were actually invented for use there

& water cannons on the streets of Brixton in 1981,
do you call that a coincidence & torture cells at Castlereagh,

sure, the Human Rights brigade found them guilty a long way back
& there are helicopters that can zoom in on yer every word.

I don't ever want to tell anyone about 'where I stand'
because I don't know myself. I tell this to the other Socialists

with their badges, rich mummies & subscriptions to 'Troops Out'.
'Have you been there? What te fuck de ye know till you've been?'

so they feel guilty then & buy me a rake of pints...

Graveside
(for my father)

A graveyard crammed with Protestants & you
all overlooking the knackered cement works

over at Magheramourne. I ride there, borrow Derm's bike
about twice a year & in some awkward phase I'm usually in

I stand & talk to your headstone, not entirely convinced
that you can hear me or that you ever do follow me around;

watch me in my city high-rise stoned, articulate then giggling
when Jo comes over & the sunset looms at Spital Tongues,

or the nights when I chat up pretty English students
in The Strawberry or when I just float about Eldon Square

trying to explain just why the city has taught me endless fear,
& let's say I've had the odd fling, the odd transgression

from the way you wanted me to be. I'm not half as gentle
as you were, nor as caring, but you can appreciate the world's changed!

So I can't keep harking back to that night in 1975
when I sat in with you cos Peg had to go to Bingo.

You asked for tea & toast coated in Lyons Golden Syrup
& it was almost as if you knew the score & felt like

a last small indulgence, a taste of what was perfect.
They came & took you to the coronary unit but I wasn't wakened

& the cardiograph they did was clear but you had them outwitted.
I was sent for in Geography & in the office Nurse Curry looked grave.

I could replay the whole scene at random & have done
& the last words I'd written in the classroom were 'broken marriages'

& Peg told me that my future plans should stay exactly the same
& I thought that was justice, I've never regretted it.

I'll never be completely English, I hope you must know that
& I do strive to be as gentle & as considerate –

at least when I blow it, get tainted by Black Bush & urges
at least I agonise over it. So if you can hear me

I'd like it if you were always nearby watching.
I've never forgotten my brother's face when Peg went to tell him.

He drew up in his Post van & she reached out to hug him.
& how I saw how his face twisted, from up in the top room.

That's imprinted on me wherever I go, this year Europe,
next year The States, today the graveside at Islandmagee.

I'm a few steps behind you, but I'm catching up...

Surrender

Singing 'yigh yigh yippie the Pope's a fuckin Hippie'
the loyal sons of Ulster used to gather in the shelter

or hog the wall near the Chinkie knee-deep in Harp tins.
They'd conspire as against my will I'd be drawn to them,

to try & get to know what makes men in bomber jackets tick,
how they see the whole shooting galllery, descendants of Planters

with names like Billy or Crawford, never Seamus or Sean.
I reckon the occupied are paranoid but so are these boys,

long after Stormont & the B-Specials they all still see it
I suppose as one long slow betrayal to London & Rome.

The 'Free State' is far from free but they're indifferent.
It's a dream they never wake from, a worse threat than Russians

& remember that boycott against buying Guinness & Fig Rolls
because they came from Dublin? It seems every 10 minutes

another reverend appears & pounds away at platforms
& there's never any faulting rhetoric if you're Orange.

Sure, what about the Clyde Valley, Carson's old gunship? –
they hauled it in glory to Carrick Harbour, then it rotted

& it's all a bit primaeval, I reckon, the uniforms & flutes,
Glasgow Rangers & hangovers, Red Hands & Ulster fries

before the long march led by men with drums & fat bellies
off to 'the field' & whatever te fuck happens there?

How should I know? It's not a football match where neutrals go,
& come to think of it I wasn't much interested in 'Our Holy Father'

when he kissed the ground at Knock. I could live without uproar
& though Westminster doesn't give a tuppenny fuck

they continue, it's their culture, well fair enough!
But I can remember a flute band stopping outside our gate,

they taunted Catholics by calling with their collection boxes
& my mother said 'don't answer' & I said I wouldn't dare

but I felt powerless & angry & bitter & frightened. Just say
one of those jokers saw me with their mates in some bar?

They might call me a Fenian Bastard, week me down by the hair,
boots gettin stuck in, it happens on both sides I know,

so when I get there, I'll stay, any place but here...